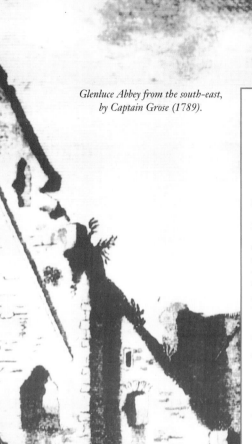

Glenluce Abbey from the south-east, by Captain Grose (1789).

Glenluce Abbey

Doreen Grove

CONTENTS	Page
INTRODUCTION	2
THE STORY OF GLENLUCE ABBEY	4
The Foundation	4
The Cistercians	6
The Medieval Years	7
Charity and Obligation	9
The Reformation	10
A SHORT TOUR OF GLENLUCE ABBEY	12
THE ABBEY AS A PLACE OF WORSHIP	14
The Church	14
The Nave	15
The Choir, Transepts and Presbytery	16
THE ABBEY AS A HOME	17
The Cloister	17
The East Range	18
The Chapter House	19
The South and West Ranges	22
CASTLE OF PARK	23
FURTHER READING	24
PLAN OF GLENLUCE ABBEY	*inside back cover*

EDITED BY CHRIS TABRAHAM
ILLUSTRATED BY DAVID SIMON & MICHELLE MCCLUSKIE
PHOTOGRAPHY BY HISTORIC SCOTLAND PHOTOGRAPHIC UNIT
PRODUCED BY ROY STEWART PRINT SERVICES
PRINTED IN SCOTLAND BY BUCCLEUCH PRINTERS LTD HAWICK

FIRST PUBLISHED BY HISTORIC SCOTLAND 1996
REPRINTED 2001
COPYRIGHT © HISTORIC SCOTLAND 1996
ISBN 1 900168 20 0

Introduction

"...in their accursed madness, finding
a monk who was at the very point
of death, lying in the infirmary of Glenlus,
they stripped him of even the sackcloth
with which he was covered"
(AN ACCOUNT, PROBABLY HIGHLY EXAGGERATED,
OF THE VENGEANCE WROUGHT BY KING ALEXANDER II'S
SOLDIERS ON GLENLUCE FOLLOWING
THE GALLOVIDIAN REVOLT OF 1235)

Glenluce Abbey was founded by Roland, Lord of Galloway, about 1192. The white-clad Cistercian monks who settled in that secluded valley of the Water of Luce most probably came from Dundrennan Abbey, near Kirkcudbright. They brought with them not only the austere way of life for which the Cistercians were renowned but also the sombre splendour of their architecture.

All too little of Glenluce Abbey survives, but hints of its former grandeur may be seen in the south transept of the church and in the chapter house. The monastic life lasted for 400 years, but because no abbey cartulary (register) has survived, our knowledge of the history of the house is almost as thin as the architectural record. We get glimpses of a community going about its spiritual and temporal life much like Cistercian monasteries elsewhere. But in the sixteenth century Glenluce had a bad press. A long-running dispute over rights to the abbey's lands eventually led, in 1560, to the monks taking up temporary exile at Maybole, in Ayrshire. The Reformation of the Scottish Church occurred at the same time, effectively ending Glenluce's days as a monastery. The 15 monks in residence at this watershed in Scottish history embraced the reformed religion in return for being allowed to live out the remainder of their days in their crumbling cloister.

Glenluce Abbey as it may have looked in the early sixteenth century; an artist's impression.

By 1602 the last monk had passed away and the abbey became a temporal lordship. But secular control did not last long. In 1619, the Diocese of Galloway, centred on Whithorn Cathedral, annexed the estate and 20 years later the old abbey re-emerged as a manse and glebe. In 1933 the abbey ruins were entrusted into State care, thereby bringing to an end almost 750 years of religious activity in this quiet Wigtownshire valley.

The Story of Glenluce Abbey

THE FOUNDATION

The very foundation of this still and peaceful monument remains obscure. The only certainty is the identity of the founder, Roland, the powerful Lord of Galloway in the last two decades of the twelfth century. After a particularly bitter conflict between the Gallovidians and the Scottish Crown during the time of his father, Uchtred, the astute Roland contrived to make the lordship strong again. The establishment of a new monastery was a demonstration of his wealth and standing in society. The choice of religious order may seem obvious to us for it was Roland's grandfather, Fergus, who had brought the white-clad Cistercian monks to the region when he founded Dundrennan Abbey in 1142. But Roland might just have easily followed the example of his wife Elena's family, the de Morevilles, who had brought the Premonstratensians to Dryburgh in the eastern Borders in 1150. Perhaps it was the proximity to Glenluce of the Premonstratensian houses at Whithorn and Soulseat that made that possibility impracticable.

A sixteenth-century drawing of Cruggleton Castle, near Garlieston, Wigtownshire, one of the chief strongholds of the Lords of Galloway.

The Cistercian abbey at Dundrennan, near Kirkcudbright, from which Glenluce may have been founded.

The date of Glenluce's foundation remains uncertain, although as a new Cistercian house it is strange that the *Chronicle* of Melrose Abbey, the premier house of the order in Scotland, is silent on the matter. Thirteenth-century lists give two dates ~ 1190 and 1192. The founding brethren probably came from the Cistercian house at Dundrennan, founded in 1142, but it is just possible that Melrose was the mother-house, for it is certainly to Melrose that the abbey looked for its abbots. In 1214, for example, Brother William, the cellarer at Melrose, was appointed abbot.

Wherever William's predecessor came from, he must have arrived in the valley of the Luce Water with at least 12 monks as was required by the Cistercian Rule. They faced the forbidding task of clearing the site and beginning the building of their great abbey. Work would have begun at the east end of the church to provide a fitting environment within which to carry out their prime function, the worship and glory of God. Once the church was well advanced, construction work would have moved on to the domestic buildings.

THE CISTERCIANS

Monasticism is almost as old as Christianity itself, and during the fifth century a monastery was established by St Ninian at Whithorn, 25 miles (40 km) south of Glenluce. Given human frailty, inevitably standards of devotion and discipline slipped, and the close of the eleventh century saw a rising tide of reforming religious zeal, with new orders hoping to return to the strict rule laid down by St Benedict in 540. The most effective of these, the Cistercians, was founded in 1098 by Robert of Molesme, at Citeaux in France, whence the name of the order. The rise of the white-clad monks was extraordinary, in part due to the efforts of the celebrated Bernard of Clairvaux. Such was his success that by the time of his death in 1153 there were 340 Cistercian houses spread across Europe.

The Cistercian rule was the harshest of all the reformed Benedictine orders. It turned its back on the world and forsook all wealth and comfort. Such was its regime of self-denial that the life-expectancy of those entering its monasteries was greatly reduced. Cistercian monasteries were sited well away from towns and areas of population, and it may be that people were evicted from the Luce valley when Glenluce was founded in 1192. In their quiet backwaters, the Cistercians dedicated themselves entirely to the silent praise of God. The emphasis was on prayer, rather than on elaborate services, and hard, physical labour. However, much of the menial work was done by *conversi*, or lay brothers, illiterate men denied the opportunity to

dedicate their lives to God in the other religious orders. They led a cloistered existence and worshipped in the abbey church, but their principal contribution to God was through hard work, either in and around the abbey precinct or on the granges, or sheep farms, which might be some distance from the abbey.

A Cistercian monk. The Cistercians were more commonly known as the 'white monks' from the colour of their habit.

The order was introduced into Scotland, to Melrose, by David I in 1136. Dundrennan followed in 1142, and Glenluce in about 1192. Roland's granddaughter, Dervorgilla, established the last Cistercian house on Scottish soil at Sweetheart, in the village of New Abbey, near Dumfries, in 1273.

THE MEDIEVAL YEARS

Glenluce never acquired the great wealth of other Cistercian houses. It did, however, hold all of Glenluce parish along with other lands in Wigtownshire and Ayrshire. The monks also had the right to purchase any goods arriving in ships entering Loch Luce and Loch Ryan. King Robert Bruce confirmed the abbey lands as a free barony in 1323 and a century later Margaret, Countess of Galloway, raised it to a Burgh of Regality.

The first abbot was *"a man of proved truthfulness and a monk of holy life"*; he also made observations on the moon. Sadly, he was considered less than exemplary by the General Chapter of the order. In 1199, after taking the advice of his father abbot at Dundrennan, he chose not to attend the General Chapter because of local unrest in Galloway. For his sins he was ordered to fast every Friday until he could come again before the Chapter the following year.

The number of monks at any one time is not known until 1560 when there were 15 in residence. The number is never likely to have risen much above that, although in the early years there were probably almost as many lay brothers as there were choir-monks. By the end of the fourteenth century the Cistercian practice of recruiting lay brethren had largely ceased, by which date the abbey's granges would have been rented to tenants.

A seal of the abbey

The history of Glenluce can only be glimpsed in contemporary charters and chronicles. Most information concerns the appointments of abbots and other officials, like the priors, cellarers, novice-masters and almoners. The promotion of monks between the houses in Scotland, northern England and Ireland was commonplace. In 1222, for instance, Abbot Adam of Holm Cultram, in Cumberland, resigned his office, to be succeeded by Ralph, Abbot of Jugum Dei, in Ireland. Ralph in turn was succeeded by Brother John, the cellarer at Glenluce, though the records are silent as to who then became

A stone basin found at the abbey. The water drained out through the fellow's mouth.

responsible for keeping the brethren at Glenluce in food and drink. The movement of personnel went beyond the order. In 1235, Gilbert, the novice-master at Melrose, was appointed Bishop of Galloway; he had previously been Abbot of Glenluce.

These were uncertain times, however, and the early abbots had more to concern them than the furthering of their careers. Supplies were difficult and in the early thirteenth century the abbot was granted permission to buy corn in Ireland for seven years. The disputed title of the lordship of Galloway following the death of Roland's son, Alan, in 1234, also affected the abbey. In 1235 the Gallovidians rose in revolt against Alexander II, who defeated them but showed "*his accustomed humanity,* [and] *extended his peace to as many as came to him; and so with ropes around their necks,* [they] *accepted his offer*". However, after he had left Galloway, some of his soldiers "*more sons of the Devil than Mars*" rampaged across the country, and "*in their accursed madness, finding a monk who was at the very point of death, lying in the infirmary of Glenlus, they stripped him of even the scrap of sackcloth with which he was covered*". Within the year, the Abbot of Glenluce had been deposed by the General Chapter, the suspicion being that he had supported those who had resisted the King.

CHARITY AND OBLIGATION

Charity and provision for travellers were obligations on all Cistercian houses. Glenluce's position on the pilgrims' way from Ayrshire to the shrine of St Ninian at Whithorn must have made this a frequent task. Robert the Bruce passed that way shortly before his death

A floor tile from the abbey decorated with horsemen.

The Laggangairn Standing Stones, at Killgallioch, on the moors north of New Luce. The stones were on a pilgrim route to Whithorn and have early Christian crosses incised on them. They are now on the Southern Upland Way and in the care of Historic Scotland.

in 1329, and James IV rested there on at least two occasions. No guest-lodging at Glenluce is identifiable, but one must have existed in the outer precinct of the abbey. Another aspect of this work was the giving of alms and succour to the poor and sick of the area. A substantial-sized infirmary, or hospital, where the monks themselves went periodically to be bled by leeches, has been identified to the east of the abbey, but it is possible that a second infirmary existed to the west of the cloister for the treatment of the lay brethren and the visiting sick. Such an obligation to its guests could cost an abbey dear. Indeed, Glenluce's unfortunate position on a major pilgrim route meant that many travellers were determined to save the lion's share of any donation they had for their final destination, Whithorn.

THE REFORMATION

The abbey survived in tolerably good strength into the sixteenth century. By this date it had acquired considerable wealth. Its abbots had become more like great landowners than spiritual leaders, and the monks themselves were most probably by now living in their own private quarters, or portions, and not together in community. This wealth made them a prey to others.

By the sixteenth century, the appointment of commendators, or administrators of an abbey's estates, had become established. These lucrative posts were often the subject of dispute. The first dispute recorded for Glenluce happened in 1514. The Battle of Flodden in the previous year had seen the deaths of many churchmen, including the Abbot of Glenluce. The ensuing vacancy was fought over by three factions. The Pope's candidate was an Italian cardinal; Walter Mallin, Bishop of Lismore, was Regent Albany's choice; and Alexander, a monk from Glenluce was the third, elected by the brethren and approved by Citeaux. In the event, Albany's candidate was successful and the poor monk was imprisoned. As it turned out, Abbot Walter proved a good choice. He brought a period of consolidation and raised standards in the abbey, bringing a scholar from Newbattle Abbey to train the novices. His zealous approach was recognised by the General Chapter when he was appointed to visit other Cistercian houses in Scotland to check on corruption and indiscipline, a task he undertook so well that the King appealed for a more lenient approach.

The interior of Maybole Collegiate Church, founded by the Kennedy family in 1373 and in which the brethren from Glenluce sheltered in the 1540s.

The outcome was a suitable compromise; the worst excesses of private profit were removed, but monks were allowed to earn their private portions.

Further disputes followed, not only at abbatial level, but between two rival noble families, the Gordons and the Kennedys. In 1544, for example, Abbot James Gordon was expelled by the Kennedy Earl of Cassillis, a compliment that was repaid when Gordon of Lochinvar evicted the brethren and occupied the property; for almost a year Cassillis gave them sanctuary in his collegiate church at Maybole, in Ayrshire. The dispute was over land and power, not religion, and was finally settled when Thomas Hay, a loyal supporter of the Earl of Cassilis and a genuine churchman, became the last abbot in 1560, the year of the Reformation. Today, even in death, the tombs of these two families vie for pole position in the abbey church.

The rise of the reform movement generated much ill-feeling in Galloway. One celebrated reformer, John McBriar, began his career as a monk at Glenluce. He was one of the few Cistercians in Galloway to accept the reformed faith, and indeed he went much further. About 1550 he was condemned for heresy and imprisoned along with Archbishop John Hamilton. He was to follow his friends and kinsmen abroad, where he spent some years writing and working in Germany. The Bishop of Galloway at the Reformation was also at heart a Protestant, though he did little to prosecute those monks at any of the three Cistercian houses in his diocese who resisted the new order. None of the 15 monks whose names are recorded in 1560 appears either as a minister, an exhorter, or a reader in the reformed Diocese of Galloway thereafter.

In 1572, Abbot Thomas and five monks were still in residence. By then almost all the lands had passed to the Earl of Cassillis, and Abbot Thomas was granted the lands of The Park, a mile to the east of the abbey, by his lord. It was his son, also Thomas, who built Castle of Park or Park Hay. For a brief time between 1602 and 1619 the abbey became a temporal lordship for the last commendator, Gordon of Lochinvar. But the abbey was bought back by the Church in 1619 for use as a manse and glebe, a position it held until the abbey came into State care in 1933.

BLISSIT·BE·THE·NAME·OF·THE·LORD·THIS
VERK·VAS·BECVN·THE·FIRST·DAY·OF·MARCH
1590·BE·THOMAS·HAY·OF·PARK·AND
JONET·MAK·DOVEL·HIS·SPOVS.

The inscription above the entrance door into Castle of Park.

A Short Tour

1. NAVE

THE LAYOUT OF THE ABBEY CHURCH FOLLOWED
THE USUAL CISTERCIAN CRUCIFORM PLAN. THE
WESTERN ARM, OR NAVE, WAS ENTERED FROM THE
WEST THROUGH THREE DOORWAYS. THE NAVE
ITSELF HAD SIX BAYS, EACH DIVIDED BY A PILLAR.
THE STONE SCREEN WALLS WERE INSERTED LATER.
THE FOUR WESTERN BAYS WERE USED BY THE LAY
BROTHERS FOR THEIR CHURCH.

2 CHOIR AND PRESBYTERY

THE REMAINDER OF THE CHURCH WAS FOR THE
EXCLUSIVE USE OF THE CHOIR-MONKS. THE HIGH
ALTAR WAS IN THE PRESBYTERY TO THE EAST. THE
CHOIR-STALLS EXTENDED WESTWARDS UNDER THE
CENTRAL CROSSING-TOWER, WHERE THE ABBEY
BELL WAS HOUSED.

3. SOUTH TRANSEPT

THE CROSS-ARMS, OR TRANSEPTS, ON EITHER SIDE
OF THE CROSSING EACH HELD TWO CHAPELS
PROVIDING ADDITIONAL ALTARS FOR THE MONKS.
THE SOUTH TRANSEPT GABLE IS THE ONLY
SUBSTANTIALLY SURVIVING CHURCH FRAGMENT. IT
CONTAINS TWO DOORS, ONE LEADING TO THE
SACRISTY, WHERE ITEMS FOR USE IN THE CHURCH
WERE STORED, AND THE OTHER TO THE
DORMITORY [SEE 5].

4. CLOISTER

AN OPEN GARDEN AROUND WHICH WERE RANGED
THE MAIN DOMESTIC QUARTERS OF THE MONKS.
THE COVERED WALK AROUND THE CLOISTER
GARTH FORMED A SHELTERED PASSAGE BETWEEN
THE VARIOUS ROOMS AS WELL AS A SPACE WHERE
THE MONKS CARRIED OUT PRIVATE READING AND
QUIET CONTEMPLATION.

5. EAST RANGE

ADJOINING THE SOUTH TRANSEPT OF THE
CHURCH, THIS RANGE HOUSED THE MOST
IMPORTANT DOMESTIC ROOMS. THESE INCLUDED
THE DORMITORY AT FIRST-FLOOR LEVEL, LINKING
DIRECTLY WITH THE CHURCH THROUGH THE
'NIGHT-STAIR', AND THE LATRINE-BLOCK AT THE
SOUTH END. THE MAIN ROOM AT GROUND LEVEL
WAS THE CHAPTER HOUSE [6].

Glenluce Abbey

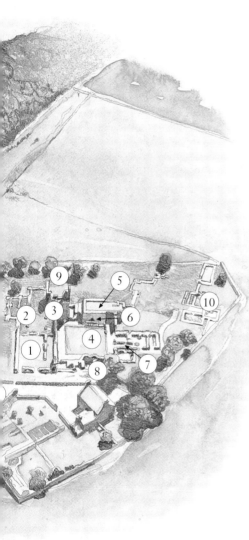

6. Chapter House

THE MOST IMPORTANT ROOM IN THE ABBEY AFTER THE CHURCH, USED BY THE BRETHREN AS THEIR MAIN MEETING-PLACE, WHERE SINS WERE CONFESSED, PUNISHMENTS METED OUT, AND IMPORTANT BUSINESS CONDUCTED. THE PRESENT CHAPTER HOUSE WAS REBUILT ABOUT 1500 AND IS THE MOST COMPLETE PART OF THE ABBEY.

7. South Range

ORIGINALLY HOUSING THE REFECTORY AND KITCHENS, BUT SUBSTANTIALLY REMODELLED IN THE 16TH CENTURY TO PROVIDE A PRIVATE RESIDENCE FOR THE ABBOT OR COMMENDATOR.

8. West Range

ORIGINALLY BUILT TO PROVIDE A DORMITORY FOR THE LAY BROTHERS ON THE FIRST FLOOR ABOVE A BASEMENT WHERE THE ABBEY'S PROVISIONS WERE STORED, BUT LATER REMODELLED TO FORM PART OF THE ABBOT'S OR COMMENDATOR'S HOUSE.

9. Site of burial Ground

THE MONKS' CEMETERY. THE ABBOTS, SENIOR OFFICIALS AND THOSE LAYMEN WHO HAD ENDOWED THE ORDER WERE INTERRED EITHER IN THE CHURCH, THE CHAPTER HOUSE, OR THE EAST CLOISTER WALK.

10. Outbuildings

SERVING A VARIETY OF USES, INCLUDING MONKS' INFIRMARY, WORKSHOPS AND STABLES.

11. Museum

AN EXHIBITION ON THE ABBEY INCLUDING A DISPLAY OF OBJECTS DISCOVERED DURING EXCAVATION WORK. AMONG THESE ARE BEAUTIFULLY DECORATED TILES AND POTTERY, AND, PERHAPS MOST IMPORTANTLY, PIPES FROM THE ABBEY'S UNUSUAL WATER-SUPPLY SYSTEM.

Artist's bird's-eye view of Glenluce Abbey from the west.

The Abbey as a Place of Worship

*W*hen the Cistercians first came to Glenluce they settled on the flat river plain of the Luce Water. The site was cleared, but seems to have needed little in the way of levelling. The plan of the abbey conforms more or less to the standard plan laid down by the order. The cruciform church was placed on the north, to ensure its great size did not shade the domestic ranges which nestled beside it. These domestic buildings were ranged around an open cloister. Beyond the church and cloister were ancillary buildings. Although the Cistercians placed great stress on austerity, the light, airy engineering of their slender pillars and lofty arcades made their churches among the most beautiful ever built.

THE CHURCH

The church was the most important building of any abbey. As the house of God within the community it was there that the monks carried out the chief work for which they had cut themselves off from the world ~ the praise and worship of the Creator. A Cistercian church had to fulfil certain needs: it had to have a presbytery to house the high altar; a choir for the monks; a nave for the lay brothers; transepts for additional altars; and plenty of room for processions which were so important to their form of worship.

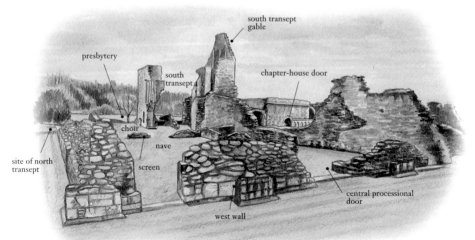

The abbey church from the west.

THE NAVE

The fragmentary remains of the aisled nave of the church are entered through what survives of the west wall. This was pierced by three **doors**, the central one leading into the nave itself and the others into each of the **side aisles**. The nave was divided into six bays with a pillar at each. The four western bays were divided off from the rest of the church by a **screen**, or pulpitum, marking the division between the lay brothers' choir and the monks' choir to the east. So little of the nave survives that it is impossible to describe the structure apart from its plan. The south wall is almost featureless and was partly rebuilt during this century.

The south transept from the central crossing.

THE CHOIR, TRANSEPTS AND PRESBYTERY

Beyond the pulpitum lay the monks' **choir**, whose wooden stalls would have run under the bell tower at the **central crossing** and into the presbytery. The only evidence for the style of the crossing is the fragmentary south-east pillar (see the photograph on page 15); with its bundled shafts and simple capitals it must have looked much like its mother-house at Dundrennan. A visitor in 1684 wrote of "*a steeple, now demolished*" over the crossing.

To north and south of the crossing were the **two transepts**. Each provided a pair of chapels on their east sides where the monks offered up private prayers. Each chapel would have had an altar with a *piscina*, or basin for washing the altar vessels, and a credence cupboard for storing the bread and wine before consecration.

The high altar stood in the simple rectangular **presbytery**, which was also doubtless similar to that at Dundrennan. In many respects, Glenluce followed the architectural style of Dundrennan, though it did not aspire to the three-storeyed splendour of its mother-house. It is also likely that the roof imitated that of Dundrennan, the main portion of the church being spanned by a timber and slate roof, while the chapels in the transepts, and perhaps the nave aisles also, were vaulted.

The remains of the **south transept** include a fragment of the wall which separated the transept from the presbytery, and the comparatively intact south gable wall. The two transept chapels along the east had quadripartite vaults and were originally divided by a timber screen. This screen was later replaced by a masonry wall (pieces of a *piscina* were built into this wall when the abbey was cleared). The church was further altered when a timber floor was inserted at the level of the vault over the transept chapels. This provided a chamber, or at least a passage, at the upper level; in so doing it blocked off the clearstory windows and was itself lit by a window in the south gable. A door at ground level led to the **sacristy**, where the vestments and other items for use in the church were stored. A second door, two metres above the ground, was part of the '**night-stair**' used by the monks for the night-time services.

The church generally was well lit and must have been an airy space. The floor throughout was covered with patterned and coloured glazed tiles, some of which are on display in the site museum (see the photographs on page 9 and 23).

The Abbey as a Home

THE CLOISTER

*T*he **processional door** at the east end of the south nave aisle opens into the cloister, a square garden edged around with a covered cloister walk and surrounded by the domestic buildings of the abbey. The cloister walk was covered with a lean-to roof sloping down from the walls of the buildings onto an open arcade. (A section of that arcade has been reconstructed along the east cloister range.) The covered walk was used for several purposes: as a passage for the brethren moving between the various rooms; as part of the processional route on special occasions; and as a place for reading and private study. The **wall-cupboard** beside the processional door stored books for this purpose.

A reconstruction of the church and cloister as it may have looked in the early sixteenth century; an artist's impression.

THE EAST RANGE

The east range of the cloister was for the exclusive use of the choir-monks. Their work was centred around the regime of services and prayers, which required them to have easy access to the church. Their **dormitory** occupied the entire upper floor of the range; the height of the roof can be seen on the gable wall of the south transept. Their individual cells may have been divided by timber screens or curtains. At the south end of the range, furthest from the church, was the **latrine-block**.

Below the dormitory on the ground floor were the abbey's main rooms. Next to the sacristy was a **slype**, or passage, leading to the monks' graveyard and infirmary beyond. To the south of the slype is the most complete room in the abbey, the chapter house (see page 19), and beyond this again another passage, probably the **inner parlour**, the only place in the abbey where necessary conversation was permitted. Beyond the parlour were the chutes serving the latrines on the upper floor.

In and around the inner parlour may be seen the remnants of the abbey's unusual **water-supply system**, runs of clay pipes interspersed at intervals by circular inspection chambers. Although the Cistercians were renowned for their engineering skills, the remains at Glenluce are a rare find.

The water pipes.

THE CHAPTER HOUSE

The chapter house was second only in importance to the church. It was here that the monks met daily to hear a reading of the chapter of the Rule governing the order, to confess their sins and receive their punishments, and to discuss other relevant business.

The east range of the cloister showing the reconstructed cloister arcading. The door to the chapter house is to the right.

The present structure was built about 1500, quite possibly in Abbot Walter's time after 1513. It is entered through a moulded and highly ornamented round-headed doorway, with an elegant and unique 'starfish' decoration on the capitals. The interior is lit from the east by two, three-light traceried windows. The glass and some of the tracery were restored during this century. The four-bay vaulting springs from decorated corbels in the walls to a central pillar. Each of the four bosses is decorated with grotesque faces around

A detail from the doorway.

The chapter-house doorway.

an armorial or centrepiece; one represents the royal arms and another the arms of a Macdowell. Around the room runs a stone bench on which the monks sat, but midway along the east wall is a more elaborate seat, emphasised by a trefoiled hood-moulding, cut from a single stone, where the abbot sat. The floor of the room was decorated with glazed tiles, and some of the originals may be seen around the pillar base.

A ceiling boss from the
chapter house carved
with the royal arms.

The interior of the chapter house
looking east towards the abbot's seat
framed by the two traceried windows.

THE SOUTH AND WEST RANGES

The **south range** originally housed the monks' refectory and kitchens but was refashioned during the sixteenth century to form a residence for the abbot or commendator. The original layout can just be traced. The **refectory**, or dining hall, was set at right angles to the cloister walk, in the normal Cistercian manner. The original entrance from the cloister walk was later blocked up and two other doorways inserted. To the east of the more easterly of these doorways was the monks' **lavatory** where they washed their hands before sitting down to their frugal vegetarian meals. The remodelling of the refectory resulted in its being converted into a two-storeyed building. In the northern half of the ground floor was a chamber with a tiled floor and a fireplace at one end, another small apartment with a latrine attached, and a small cell entered directly from the cloister walk. In the southern half were two barrel-vaulted chambers, the outer one apparently a **brewhouse**. To the west of the refectory was the **kitchen**.

To the south of the range are the remains of **outbuildings** of uncertain date and function.

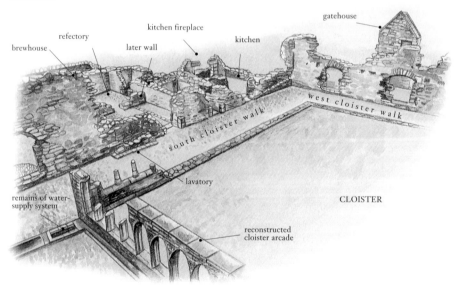

The south and west ranges.

As originally planned, the west range would have provided domestic quarters for the lay brothers, more or less echoing the provision for the choir-monks in the east range. It is not clear when the presence of lay-brethren dwindled, but the present buildings in the range, the line of vaulted **cellars** and the rather intriguing **gatehouse** which remains roofed, were built in the sixteenth century to form part of the new residence.

A floor tile from the abbey decorated with a crozier.

CASTLE OF PARK

The tall stark tower house which stands sentinel over the entrance to the valley of the Luce Water was built by Thomas Hay, son of the last Abbot of Glenluce, in 1590. The estate had been acquired by his father from the Earl of Cassillis. The castle is now privately managed but can be viewed from the outside.

The L-plan tower house has four floors and a garret. The entrance doorway in the re-entrant angle is protected by a small gun-hole. Above the doorway is a dated inscription to Thomas Hay and his wife, Jonet Macdowell (see page 11). On the ground floor is a roomy kitchen, reached from along a passage off which are two other cellars, one of them a wine cellar with a back-stair leading to the hall on the floor above. The main access to the hall and to the upper floors is up a sweeping stair in the projecting wing of the tower house.

The hall occupied most of the first floor. It was the family's principal living room and served also as the dining room; the fireplace has a simple grandeur. The hall would originally have been screened off at the entrance end by a timber partition. At the opposite end there was a small private chamber and an additional stair giving private access to the upper floors which provided private rooms for the lord and his family. Around the castle were gardens and parkland. The house remained in the ownership of the Hay family until the 1830s, when *"everything portable was removed to Dungrait"*, or Dunragit, another of their residences.

Castle of Park in 1950.

Further Reading

ON THE ABBEY:
R Fawcett *Scottish Medieval Churches* (1985)
R Reid *Wigtownshire Charters* Scottish History Society third series, LI (1960)

ON THE CISTERCIANS GENERALLY:
P Fergusson *The Architecture of Solitude* (1984)
R Fawcett *Scottish Abbeys and Priories* (1994)
M Dilworth *Scottish Monasteries in the Late Middle Ages* (1995)
D Robinson (ed.) *The Cistercian Abbeys of Britain* (1998)

ON GALLOWAY GENERALLY:
R Oram and G Stell *Galloway Land and Lordship* (1991)
D Brooks *Wild Men and Holy Places* (1994)